Robert Burns: Reflections of an Age

Dumfries and Galloway Libraries
1995

Robert Burns: Reflections of an Age

First published 1995
© Copyright Dumfries and Galloway Libraries

All rights reserved. No part of this publication may be reproduced, stored in a retrieval system, or transmitted, in any form or by any means, electronic, mechanical, photocopying, recording or otherwise, without the prior permission of Dumfries and Galloway Libraries.

Designed and set by Dumfries and Galloway Libraries. Printed by Solway Offset Services, Catherinefield Industrial Estate, Dumfries, for the publisher.

Dumfries and Galloway Libraries
Catherine Street
Dumfries DG1 1JB

Dumfries and Galloway
LIBRARIES

ISBN 0946280 17 7

For a full list of our publications write to the above address.

Robert Burns: Reflections of an Age

Introduction

This publication has been compiled by Dumfries and Galloway Libraries to commemorate the bicentenary of the death of Robert Burns.

The eighteenth century was a period of great change. The Scottish people felt the consequences of the Act of Union of 1707, the end of the clan system and Jacobitism and the decline of Calvinism; they participated in the agricultural and industrial revolutions and witnessed the great political revolutions overseas, fuelled by demands for democratic government and rights for individuals.

Robert Burns experienced the aftermath of some of these changes and lived through many of them. At a time when it was dangerous for the 'ordinary' man to express opinions on politics, religion or philosophy, Burns proclaimed the rights of man, denounced hypocrisy and oppression and championed the cause of freedom.

Excerpts from the poet's verses and letters (reproduced with original spellings) are combined with illustrations and articles, many from contemporary sources, to provide background information and an introduction to some of the events, people and places which influenced his life and work.

JHG

He'll hae misfortunes great and sma',
But ay a heart aboon them a';
He'll be a credit till us a',
We'll a' be proud o' Robin.

Key Dates

1707	Act of Union Ratification of Presbyterian Constitution of the Kirk of Scotland
1715	Jacobite rising
1733	Jethro Tull publishes *The horse hoeing husbandry*, which advocated new agricultural methods
1739	Publication of Hume's *Treatise of human nature*
1745	Jacobite rising
1746	Jacobites defeated at Culloden
1748	Publication of Hume's *Enquiry concerning human understanding*
1759	**Birth of Robert Burns**
1760	Accession of George III
1762	Publication of Rousseau's *Le contract social*
1763	Treaty of Paris, end of Seven Years war
1766	**The Burns family move to Mount Oliphant farm**
1769	Watt invents the steam engine
1770	Boston massacre
1772	First partition of Poland between Russia, Prussia and Austria
1773	Revolution led by Pugachov in Russia "Boston Tea Party"
1775	First action in American War of Independence at Lexington
1776	American Declaration of Independence Publication of Smith's *Wealth of nations*
1777	Surrender of British army to Americans at Saratoga
1777	**The Burns family move to Lochlea**
1779	Death of James Cook
1781	Surrender of British to American and French forces
1783	Britain recognises American independence Pitt becomes prime minister
1784	Introduction of the mail coach system
1784	**Robert and Gilbert become the tenants of Mossgiel**
1786	**Publication of Kilmarnock edition** **Burns goes to Edinburgh**
1787	Constitution of the United States drawn up
1787	**Publication of Edinburgh edition**
1788	**Burns marries Jean Armour** **Burns' Excise Commission issued** **Burns takes the lease of Ellisland Farm**
1789	George Washington becomes first President of the United States of America French revolution begins. Storming of the Bastille
1791	Publication of Paine's *Rights of man*
1791	**Burns moves to Dumfries**
1792	France becomes a Republic
1793	Louis XVI beheaded Second partition of Poland Declaration of war by French Republic on Allies, including Britain
1794	"Glorious First of June" Fall of Robespierre and end of Jacobin republic
1795	Napoleon Bonaparte disperses Paris mob
1796	**Death of Robert Burns**
1797	Treaty of Campo Formio - Bonaparte compels Austria to make peace, leaving Britain to fight France alone

Robert Burns: Reflections of an Age

Contents

Introduction	page v
Key Dates	page vi
Farming	page 1
Religion	page 9
Freemasons	page 17
Women	page 25
Edinburgh	page 33
Excise	page 41
Revolution	page 49
Dumfries	page 57
Sources	page 66

Robert Burns: Reflections of an Age

Farming

"My father was a farmer..."

Colonel Fullarton, in a "General View of Ayrshire" drawn up in 1793, says, that in the middle of the eighteenth century there was scarcely a practicable road in the whole county. The farm-houses were mere hovels, coated with clay, having an open hearth or fire-place in the middle of the floor, a dunghill at the door, the cattle starving, and the people wretched. The land was overrun with weeds and rushes, and was gathered into high, broad, and serpentine ridges. The soil was collected on the centre of each ridge, and the furrows were generally drowned in water. There was no drainage, no fallows, no green crops, no sown grass, no carts or waggons, no straw-yards; hardly a potato or any esculent root; few garden vegetables, except Scotch kail, which with milk and oatmeal formed the main diet of the people. The farmers were in the habit of yoking four horses to each plough, which was constructed of the strongest and clumsiest materials, and there was a man to hold, another to drive, and a third to clear the mould-board and to keep the coulter in the ground. The supernumerary, who seems to have been peculiar to Ayrshire, carried a pole about six feet long, the end of which was fixed to the point of the ploughbeam by a hook and fork, so that he could either push the plough towards the furrow, if the slice was too broad, or drag it towards the land if too narrow, and this practice continued till 1770.

Colonel Fullarton also informs us that markets for agricultural produce were so low, and public credit so ill established, that no tenant was able to raise money enough to stock his farm properly, and few landowners had the means of improving their estates. There were no manufactures in the country, except a small trade in bonnets at Stewarton, and in shoes and carpets at Kilmarnock. Exports and imports at Ayr, Irvine, and Saltcoats were on a very small scale, and some of the finest lands in the county were let for a few shillings per acre. There was neither skill, industry, capital, nor credit; and if the season proved unfavourable, a dearth or famine generally ensued.

In these seasons of misery the poor people were frequently obliged to " subsist by bleeding their cattle and mixing the blood with what oatmeal they could procure."

In ordinary times very little butcher meat was used, except a proportion which every family salted at Martinmas to serve during winter with their groats, barley, and greens; the rest of the food consisted chiefly of porridge and milk or sowens, oatmeal cakes, and cheese.

At the same period, as we are told by Aiton in his "View of Ayrshire," the farm-houses were
" despicable hovels; many of them were built in part, and some altogether of turf, or of mud plastered on stakes and basket-work." Clay mixed with cut straw was used as mortar, and the roof was formed of strong couples about eight feet apart, fixed into the walls, and reaching to a point near the ground. Beams of wood stretched across to unite each couple, and on these rested wings or cabbers about the thickness of a man's arm. Brushwood, sods, and straw came next, and the " Clay-bigging" was complete. But the doors were seldom more than five feet high, and the windows about eighteen inches square, into which panes of glass or dealboards were fixed in frames, to be opened and shut at pleasure. "That part of the building," says Aiton, "which served the family for lodging, sleeping, cooking, eating, and dairy purposes, was denominated the 'inseat,' and was about twelve or fourteen feet square, with the fire in the centre of the floor or at the gable, without jambs or smoke-funnel. On large farms another apartment, of nearly the same dimensions, which entered through the inseat, was called the 'spense,' in which were stored the meal chest, the sowen tub, some beds, a cask in which the urine was collected, called the wash tub, besides spinning-wheels and reels when not in use, and the gudewife's press, if she had one. The other part of the building was occupied by the cattle, which generally entered by the same door with the family; the one turning to the one hand by the 'trans-door' to the kitchen, and through it to the 'spense,' and the other turning the contrary way, by the 'keek' door, to the byre or stable. The 'trans' and 'keek' doors were in the centre of the partitions, so that the people in the 'inseat' or kitchen saw butt to the byre, and the cattle of course saw ben to the kitchen. A causeway, about six feet broad, formed of large stones carelessly laid down, ran between the two doors to the 'fore' or outer door of the building, and immediately in front of the latter was the dungstead with its accompanying cesspool; and all round the building were sinks and gutters for the reception of the urine from the byre, and all the refuse or offal from the dairy and kitchen. Strangers in those days 'scented' the farm-houses afar off; but if they attempted to reach them without a guide after nightfall, they were fortunate if they succeeded without sinking to the knees in mud, manure, or putrid matter."

(1) Tytler's History of Scotland, c1850

My father was a farmer upon the Carrick border O
And carefully he bred me, in decency and order O
He bade me act a manly part, though I had ne'er a farthing O
For without an honest manly heart, no man was worth regarding. O

Then out into the world my course I did determine. O
Tho' to be rich was not my wish, yet to be great was charming. O
My talents they were not the worst; nor yet my education: O
Resolv'd was I, at least to try, to mend my situation. O

In many a way, and vain essay, I courted fortune's favor; O
Some cause unseen, still stept between, and frustrate each endeavor; O
Some times by foes I was o'erpower'd; sometimes by friends forsaken; O
And when my hope was at the top, I still was worst mistaken. O

Then sore harass'd, and tir'd at last, with fortune's vain delusion; O
I dropt my schemes, like idle dreams; and came to this conclusion; O
The past was bad, and the future hid; its good or ill untryed; O
But the present hour was in my pow'r, and so I would enjoy it, O

No help, nor hope, nor view had I; nor person to befriend me; O
So I must toil, and sweat and moil, and labor to sustain me, O
To plough and sow, to reap and mow, my father bred me early, O
For one, he said, to labor bred, was a match for fortune fairly, O

Thus all obscure, unknown, and poor, thro' life I'm doom'd to wander, O
Till down my weary bones I lay in everlasting slumber; O
No view nor care, but shun whate'er might breed me pain or sorrow; O
I live today as well's I may, regardless of tomorrow, O

But cheerful still, I am as well as a Monarch in a palace; O
Tho' fortune's frown still hunts me down with all her wonted malice: O
I make indeed, my daily bread, but ne'er can make it farther; O
But as daily bread is all I heed, I do not much regard her. O

All you who follow wealth and power with unremitting ardor, O
The more in this you look for bliss, you leave your view the farther; O
Had you the wealth Potosi boasts, or nations to adore you, O
A chearful honest-hearted clown I will prefer before you. O

'My father was a farmer'

During the last quarter of the century a vast improvement took place both in the methods of farming and in the domestic accommodation and mode of living of the agricultural classes, and the best effects resulted from the mechanical improvements of husbandry, and from superior skill and dexterity in the use of them. The mean, small, inconvenient houses of the farmer, consisting of one story, with the rooms often not floored, were replaced by handsome and comfortable residences, and the dirty unhealthy stables and byres, by offices arranged for convenience and comfort. Hedging, ditching, planting, and improving converted barren moors and mosses into fruitful arable and pasture land. "The beautiful hedgerows," says Mr. Struthers, "the thriving clumps, and the convenient inclosures of one proprietor, excited the taste and awakened the emulation of another, till hands could with difficulty be found to execute, or sufficiency of materials to complete, the improvements that were in progress; while each, astonished at the beauty and fertility that so suddenly began to grow around him, was anxious to engage in new and still more extensive experiments. These rapid improvements necessarily produced a remarkable change in the habits of the people, and in all their modes of operation. Negligence and sloth gave place to patient industry and careful economy. The cumbrous and inefficient implements of husbandry, so long handed down from one generation to another without any attempts either at alteration or improvement, now fell into disuse; and practices, evidently the offspring of indolence, were laid aside. With ploughs of a lighter make and a more happy construction, one man and two horses performed the work that formerly required two men and four horses. Taught by experience the value of manure, the farmer no longer employed the mountain torrent to clean out his dunghill, under the pretence of enriching some small portion of meadow land over which, in careless manner, that mountain torrent for a part of the year had been turned. He now knew better how to husband that to him necessary article, and the greater quantity he could collect against the coming seed-time, so much richer he foresaw would be the coming harvest. His crop was no longer raised in patches scattered over a naked farm, a patch here and a patch there, with a ragged boy chasing a few half-starved cattle up and down among them from morning till night. He now cropped an entire inclosure, which, if not skilfully, was at least diligently cultivated, and promised him a reasonable return, while in another he pastured his cattle, all of the fine milking Ayrshire breed."

For the cheese, butter, and butter-milk, which his cows produced, he had always a ready market, either among the neighbouring villagers or at some of the public works in the neighbourhood, or in the cities and towns adjacent - a source of profit to the farmer which might in some respects be said to be entirely new, and which in many instances amounted to a sum larger than what he was accustomed to draw for the produce of his whole farm. It is no matter of surprise that, as Dr. Somerville states, a good many tenants made so much money by farming, even in those days, as to be enabled to purchase estates.

The change which took place in a rural parish in the neighbourhood of Glasgow may be taken as a fair average specimen of the improvements in the cultivation of the soil, and in the enterprise of the farmers throughout the Lowland districts of the country. "In 1750 the land rent of the parish did not exceed £1000. In 1790 the land rent rose to £2850. In 1750 every farm was distinguished into croft and field land. The former, which seldom exceeded a fifth of the whole, lay near the farm-house, was frequently manured, and constantly in tillage; the latter, which lay at a distance from the farm-house, was never manured, but sometimes in tillage, though oftener in pasture.
In 1790 the distinction between croft and field land was entirely abolished, and every part of the farm treated in the same manner. In 1750 most of the farms run-rig, that is, the lands of one farmer intermixed with those of another. No inclosures but a very few about gentlemen's houses. Every field contained a number of balks or waste places between the ridges, full of stones and bushes. The ridges curved very high in the middle, and often unequal in breadth. In 1790 all the farms divided, and some of them subdivided, with hawthorn hedges. No 'balks' now to be seen; the whole field cultivated. The ridges straight, reduced to a proper swell in the middle, and to a regular breadth."

By the end of the century an increase had taken place in the rent and price of the land, corresponding to the great improvement which had been made in the mode of cultivating the soil. In the course of the last half of the century the rent increased generally threefold, in some instances fourfold, and in few instances less than a hundred per cent.; the price of land of course advanced in a corresponding proportion. In the Lowlands it was not at all uncommon to find estates yielding thirty per cent. in the shape of rent on the original price at which they were purchased sixty years before.

(2) Tytler's History of Scotland, c1850

My father's generous master died; the farm proved a ruinous bargain; and, to clench the curse, we fell into the hands of a Factor who sat for the picture I have drawn of one in my Tale of two dogs... My father was advanced in life ... and worn out by early hardship, was unfit for labour ...We lived very poorly; I was a dextrous ploughman for my years... My indignation yet boils at the recollection of the scoundrel tyrant's insolent, threatening epistles, which used to set us all in tears

Letter from Burns to Dr John Moore, 1787

(3) Mount Oliphant farm. Tenanted by the Burns family from 1766 to 1777

Agriculture—has made great progress here, as well as in other parts of the country, within the last thirty or forty years. The lands of Alloway, being the full half of the present country parish of Ayr, were formerly possessed by tenants at the yearly rent of 1s. 3d. per acre, which they were not able to pay, and often became bankrupts and beggars. In the year 1755, these lands were sold by the town to private proprietors, who continue to pay the antient rent as a perpetual feu-duty, and the sale produced a capital of L.7200. Since that period, the lands have been brought into good cultivation, and are now finely inclosed, and adorned with plantations and country seats

(4) Ayr Parish
First Statistical Account, 1790s

Poor tenant-bodies, scant o' cash,
How they maun thole a factor's snash;
He'll stamp an' threaten, curse an' swear,
He'll apprehend them, poind their gear,
While they maun stand, wi' aspect humble,
An' hear it a', an' fear an' tremble!

from 'The twa dogs'

(5) The Burns family moved to Lochlea farm, Tarbolton in 1777

Agriculture.—Barley and *oats* are the prevalent articles of grain-crop. The lands are carefully fubdivided and inclofed, here and there with hedge-rows of trees and belts of planting. *Potatoes* are the principal article of green crop; among other varieties of the potatoe, there is particularly a beautiful long white one, very advantageoufly in ufe here. The gardens afford abundance of pulfe and pot-herbs. The *climate* is here, as around this weftern coaft in general, moift, and fubject to frequent rains. Yet it is fufficiently genial; for in the middle of September in the year 1795, the harveft was more than one half advanced. The *foil* is a reddifh loam; and here and there are confiderable ftrata of *peat*-earth. The culture of *turnips*, as a crop for forage and for fallowing, is not yet fully eftablifhed in this parifh; but begins to be continually more and more adopted.

(6) Tarbolton Parish
First Statistical Account, 1790s

We are much at a loss for want of proper methods in our improvements of farming: necessity compels us to leave our old schemes; and few of us have opportunities of being well informed in new ones.

Letter from Burns to his cousin, 1783

I entered on this farm with full resolution, "Come, go to, I will be wise!"- I read farming books; I calculated crops; I attended markets... but the first year from unfortunately buying in bad seed, the second from a late harvest, we lost half of both our crops.

Letter from Burns to Dr John Moore, 1787

(7) Mossgiel farm, Mauchline
Tenanted by Robert Burns
and his brother Gilbert in 1784

The foil in the parish, is, for the moſt part, of a clayiſh nature, except ſome fields, about Machlin, which are of a light ſandy, or mixt kind. Hence, the ſame weather does not ſuit both; and, when there is a good crop on the one, there is a light or bad crop on the other.—The whole of this pariſh is arable, except two ſmall moſſes, and ſome declivities on the banks of the Ayr, fit for planting. A large tract of land, called Machlin-muir, has, of late years, been turned into arable land, and properly incloſed and ſurrounded with belts of planting, by the late Sir Thomas Miller. In general, all the lands or farms in the pariſh, within theſe 40 or 50 years, have been incloſed and ſubdivided.

(8) Mauchline Parish
First Statistical Account, 1790s

November chill blaws loud wi' angry sugh;
    The short'ning winter-day is near a close;
The miry beasts retreating frae the pleugh;
    The black'ning trains o' craws to their repose:
The toil-worn Cotter frae his labor goes,
    This night his weekly moil is at an end,
Collects his spades, his mattocks and his hoes,
    Hoping the morn in ease and rest to spend,
And weary, o'er the muir, his course does hameward bend.

from 'The Cotter's Saturday Night'

I have at last taken a lease of a farm. Yesternight I completed a bargain with Mr Miller, of Dalswinton, for the farm of Ellisland on the banks of the Nith, between five and six miles above Dumfries. I begin at Whitsunday to build a house, drive lime, &c and heaven be my help! for it will take a strong effort to bring my mind into the routine of business.

Letter from Burns to Margaret Chalmers, 1788

(9) Ellisland farm, Dunscore Parish
Leased by Burns in 1788

Cattle and sheep.—The number of black cattle is nearly 1300; the number of sheep 3480; and the number of horses 218. The black cattle, in general, are of the Galloway breed; but Mr Robert Burns, a gentleman well known by his poetical productions, who rents a farm in this parish, is of opinion, that the west country cows give a larger quantity of mi...

Agriculture and produce.—This parish, besides supplying itself with provisions, exports oats, meal, and barley. Hemp and flax are not much cultivated, though more has been raised of late than formerly; and, in the course of the ensuing season, a flax-mill is to be erected on the river Cairn. Oats are sown in March and April, and reaped in September and October. Barley is sown in the beginning of May. There are about 72 ploughs in the parish, and chiefly of the Scottish kind.

(10) Dunscore Parish, First Statistical Account, 1790s

Robert Burns: Reflections of an Age

Religion

"*O Thou that in the heavens does dwell...*"

Ecclesiastical authority over the morals of the community was wielded in the early part of the century with almost undisputed sway. The lynx eyes of elders and deacons, appointed both to watch and pray, were alert in every corner. Every rumour, every suspicion of ill-doing was reported to the Kirk-Session, and evidence of the most inquisitive kind was taken; and if the inquiry was too delicate even for elders, matrons were appointed to examine and give their testimony. Immorality was rife in spite of the terror of the Church, and culprits had to pay their fines graduated according to the heinousness and frequency of the offence. Offenders stood "at the pillory"- a raised platform or a stool in front of the pulpit, clad in a cloak of sackcloth, which they might be obliged to buy or make for themselves - and there to be admonished by the minister until he was satisfied of their penitence. For gravest scandals persons were required to appear many Sundays in succession, when they went through the terrible ordeal of facing the congregation, and receiving rebukes from the minister.

Contumacy and refusal to obey the orders of Presbytery to stand rebuke incurred the dread sentence of greater excommunication, - this involved the mysterious "being delivered over to Satan", banishment from the church and denial of its sacraments. This rendered the delinquent an outcast from society, marked him with the brand of infamy, and was so potent a judgement that the most obdurate often gave in at last, and consented to give whatever "satisfaction" was demanded. The Church had far reaching powers, for if a suspected person refused to compear before the Presbytery it called in the authority of the sheriff; and even if a delinquent refused to take the rebuke except from his seat, ecclesiastical authorities threatened that they would apply to the magistrates to compel him to stand "at the pillar".

To have carried a pair of shoes on a Fast Day, to have whistled, or walked on the roads, and pulled a turnip in the garden, incurred heavy censure, a fine or appearance in the pillory. Even to have carried a can of water to a sick person was treated as a profanation of the Sabbath, and the use of hasty words in which "devil" or "God" was wantonly uttered, was matter of grave inquiry and sessional discipline.

No more common source of hurt to good morals existed in those days than the favourite gatherings at "penny weddings". The rural classes in those gloomy days had few social pleasures, and what they had were forbidden ones. They were extremely poor; they had no means wherewith to furnish forth the entertainment at a bridal; and it was the custom of the country for friends and neighbours to subscribe money - originally - one penny each - to provide food, drink and fiddler. Scandals undoubtedly attended these gatherings; drinking, rioting and immorality were the constant accompaniments and consequences. The General Assembly passed stringent Acts against "promiscuous dancing"; Kirk-Sessions attacked those meetings and all who took part in them - musicians and dancers alike.

Many other matters came under the cognisance of the ever busy ecclesiastical authorities. Most conspicuous of these were charges of "trafficking with Satan". Superstition was spread amongst all classes; there was not an event of their lives, from birth to death, which was free from it. Witchcraft, above all, was looked upon with horror and profound belief in the first quarter of the century. Every whisper of the "trafficking with Satan" was heard with awful eagerness, and evidence was brought to the Kirk-Session of every suspicious circumstance.

In those days there was oversight exercised in every part of existence and every day of man's life. Every night, at nine o'clock or ten o'clock, elders went through the streets to see if any one loitered on the way; they entered the taverns and dismissed the occupants home. Yet in spite of all precautions there were frequent clamant complaints by Synods and Town Councils at the deplorable condition of society - "at the abounding vice, immorality, particularly horrid swearing, breach of the Lord's Day, drunkenness, uncleanness, mocking at religion and religious exercises". Whether these tirades were due to the over-scrupulosity of the pious or really to the wickedness of the people, it is difficult to decide.

An unpleasant feature in these olden days of discipline is the inequality of the sentences. There was a leniency to the rich which was not shown to the poor. This inequality was not always due to the clergyman - who might be impartial enough - but to the elders who, if not fellow lairds, were tenants on his ground or dependent on his favour, and feared to incur his displeasure.

These inquisitions did vastly more harm than good. They were dangerous weapons to put in the hands of every malcontent who had a grudge to gratify or a fanatical grievance to express, with the risk of making a clergyman's life a burden to him and his congregation a terror. As the century went on these old visitations were gradually dropped, as they were found to be mere sources of trouble and discontent, interesting only to busybodies in the Church courts and grumblers in the pews.

(11) Social Life in Scotland in the Eighteenth Century, 1909

I have already appeared publickly in Church, and was indulged in the liberty of standing in my own seat.

Letter from Burns to Mr David Brice, 1786

> Newabbey 17th May 1790 P.P. Sedt &c
> John Douglas in Midglen & Nicolas Wauch
> his servant, Owned an Irregular Marriage
> they were rebuked & absolved - & He paid a
> fine of 20 sh - which was applied to the sal-
> lary of the school above the Wood
>
> Douglas & Wauch

(12) Extract from New Abbey Kirk Session Records

During the period from 1707 to 1750 there was quietly going on a movement which was slowly disintegrating the austere, fanatic religious character of Scotland. This movement was the growth of interest and employment in trade which arose some years after the Union with England. Industries began to give occupation to the people; the linen and woollen trade began to take up their attention; foreign trade in time gave outlets for their energy abroad as manufactures did at home; and later in the century agricultural improvements gave new interests to their minds. So long as there was social stagnation their thoughts remained in the old grooves. But men congregated in towns were less under the inquisition of the churches; they discussed material concerns more and sacred things less, and old spiritual matters fell out of sight as ministerial supervision fell off. Fuller intercourse with the world rubbed off many a prejudice; just as Scotsmen changed their fashions of working and of dressing, they changed their ways of thinking too. If this took place amongst the lower classes, it took place with much more rapidity amongst the educated orders. Closer communication with England, the increase of business, the presence in Parliament of sixty representative gentry and nobles, their residence with their families in the south; were amongst the means which brought new notions of all things, of gardening and farming, new modes of dress and new manners of living, fresher knowledge of literature and wider views in religion.

Two parties now stood forth in the Church - the "legal" preachers or moralists and the "high-flyers" or evangelicals. They were hotly opposed to each other, and the debates in Church courts became sources of intense enjoyment to the idle men of Edinburgh, who would say, "Come, let us go and see sport at the Assembly".

After the middle of the century toleration, spread amongst all classes, had leavened the ranks of the clergy, over whose manners and tone a vast change had passed. Even the Evangelical party - strict and austere as they were - were unable to resist the tide of new feeling which had come over the age: they were more genial in faith and more cheerful in life.

Evangelical ministers of the old school still abounded in the Church to leaven the arid Moderatism, their teaching drearily doctrinal, their discipline still severe and vigilant; yet from the finer Evangelical clergy came teaching which in its mild tone and benign spirit was a strange contrast to that of an older generation.

(13) Social Life in Scotland in the Eighteenth Century. 1909

Robert Burns: Reflections of an Age

> Rob.t Burns was born at Alloway in the Parish of Ayr — Jan.y 25.th 1759 —
>
> Jean Armour his wife was born at Mauchline Feb.y 27.th 1767 —
>
> Sept.r 3, 1786 there born to them twins, Robert, their eldest son, at a quarter past Noon, & Jean, since dead at fourteen months old. — March 3, 1788 were born to them twins again, two daughters, who died within a few days after their birth. — August 18th 1789 was born to them, Francis Wallace; so named after Mrs Dunlop of Dunlop; he was born a quarter before seven, forenoon. — April 9th 1791, between three & four in the morning, was born to them William Nicol; so named after Will.m Nicol of the High School, Edin.r — November 21.st 1792, at a quarter past Noon, was born to them Elizabeth Riddel, so named after Mrs Rob.t Riddel of Glenriddel.
>
> James Glencairn born 12th Aug.t 1794 named after the late Earl of Glencairn.
>
> Maxwell Born 26.th July 1796 the day of his Father's Funeral; named after Dr. Maxwell the Physician who attended the Poet in his last illness. Inserted by W. N. Burns 9.th April 1867.

(14) Burns' Bible: The family register

Religion

> *But I gae mad at their grimaces,*
> *Their sighan, cantan, grace-prood faces,*
> *Their three-mile prayers, an 'hauf-mile graces,*
> *Their raxan conscience,*
> *Whase greed, revenge, an' pride disgraces*
> *Waur nor their nonsense.*
>
> *from 'Epistle to John McMath'*

Calvinism, at that time, was agitated with a schism among its professors, and the factions were known in the west by the names of Old Light and New Light. The Old Light enthusiasts aspired to be ranked with the purest of the Covenanters; they patronized austerity of manners and humility of dress, and stigmatized much that the world loved, as things vain and unessential to salvation. The New Light countenanced no such self-denial; men were permitted to gallop on Sunday, to make merry and enjoy themselves; and women were indulged in the article of dress, and failings or follies were treated with mercy at least, if not indulgence. The former refused to lean on the slender reed of human works, thought a good deed savoured of selfishness, and that faith, and faith alone, was the light which led to heaven: the latter thought cheerful heart was an acceptable thing with God; that good works helped to make a good end, and that faith, and faith alone, was not religion, but a false light, which led to perdition. Like the writers in the late singular controversy on Art and Nature in Poetry, the divines of the west of Scotland perhaps never concluded that faith and works were both essential to salvation, and that, in truth, Christianity required them. Each side thundered from the pulpit; their sermons partook of the character of curses, and their conversation in private life had the hue of controversy. Their parishioners, too, raised up their voices—for, in Scotland, the meanest peasant can be eloquent and puzzling on speculative theology—and the whole land rung with mystical discussions on effectual calling, free grace, and predestination

(15) Complete Works of Robert Burns

> *O Gowdie, terror o' the whigs,*
> *Dread o' black coats and reverend wigs!*
> *Sour Bigotry on his last legs*
> *Girns and looks back,*
> *Wishing the ten Egyptian plagues*
> *May sieze you quick.*
>
> *from 'Epistle to John Goldie'*

Orthodox, Orthodox, who believe in John Knox,
    Let me sound an alarm to your conscience;
A heretic blast has been blawn i' the West
    That what is not Sense must be Nonsense, Orthodox,
    That what is not Sense must be Nonsense.

Doctor Mac, Doctor Mac, ye should streek on a rack,
    To strike Evildoers with terror;
To join FAITH and SENSE upon any pretence
    Was heretic, damnable error, etc.

Calvin's Sons, Calvin's Sons, seize your spiritual guns
    Ammunition ye never can need;
Your HEARTS are the stuff will be POWDER enough,
    And your SCULLS are a storehouse o' LEAD, etc.

from 'The Kirk's alarm'

Wee ****** niest, the guard relieves,
    An' Orthodoxy raibles,
Tho' in his heart he weel believes,
    An' thinks it auld wives' fables:
But faith! the birkie wants a Manse,
    So, cannilie he hums them;
Altho' his carnal Wit an' Sense
    Like hafflins-wise o'ercomes him
        At times that day.

His piercin words, like highlan swords,
    Divide the joints an' marrow;
His talk o' H-ll, whare devils dwell,
    Our vera 'Sauls does harrow'
        Wi' fright that day.

A vast, unbottom'd boundless Pit,
    Fill'd fou o' lowan brunstane,
Whase raging flame, an' scorching heat,
    Wad melt the hardest whunstane!

from 'The holy fair'

(16) Part of the MS of 'Holy Willie's Prayer'

(17) Holy Willie

(18) 'Let us worship God'

Compar'd with this, how poor Religion's pride,
  In all the pomp of method and of art,
When men display to congregations wide
  Devotion's ev'ry grace, except the heart!
The Power, incens'd, the Pageant will desert,
  The pompous strain, the sacerdotal stole;
But haply, in some cottage far apart,
  May hear, well pleas'd, the language of the soul;
And in His Book of Life the Inmates poor enroll.

from 'The Cotter's Saturday Night'

Robert Burns: Reflections of an Age

Freemasons

"May secresy round be the mystical bound"

Robert Burns: Reflections of an Age

On November 30, 1736, the first general assembly of symbolic masons was held, and a grand lodge for Scotland formed. The representative of the St Clair family then resigned his hereditary office and was elected first grand master. St Andrew's day was substituted for the day of St John the Baptist. Provincial grand masters were soon added, and there was a general adhesion of Scotch lodges to the new organization. The subsequent history of the brotherhood is not eventful. In Scotland they have been more remarkable for conviviality, or "refreshment," as it is technically called, than for comprehensive charity. Their gloves, aprons, sashes, and jewels are well known in festival or funeral processions. Their political relations have been peaceful.

In 1800, when intercourse with some Irish regiments had introduced the templar degrees to some of the Ayrshire lodges, an attempt was made by the law officers of the crown to convict certain templars at Maybole of sedition and the administration of unlawful oaths. The case only resulted in the disclosure of the extremely absurd ceremonies connected with the two degrees of this royal order, one of them consisted in drinking porter out of a human skull. In 1811 a supreme grand royal arch chapter of Scotland was founded at Edinburgh, but its degrees were denounced and have never been recognized by the grand lodge.
Scotland has altogether 400 lodges.

(19) Encyclopædia Britannica, 1875

I went to a Mason-lodge yesternight where the Most Worshipful Grand Master Charters, and all the Grand Lodge of Scotland visited. The meeting was most numerous and elegant; all the different Lodges about town were present in all their pomp. The Grand Master who presided with great solemnity, and honor to himself as a Gentleman and Mason, among other general toasts gave, "Caledonia, & Caledonia's Bard, brother B----," which rung through the whole Assembly with multiplied honors and repeated acclamations. As I had no idea such a thing would happen, I was downright thunderstruck, and trembling in every nerve made the best return in my power. Just as I finished, some of the Grand Officers said so loud as I could hear, with a most comforting accent, "Very well indeed!" which set me something to rights again.

Letter from Burns to John Ballantine, 1787

The most distinguished name on the roll of Scottish Freemasonry is that of Robert Burns, and members of the Ancient and Honourable Fraternity must ever regard it as an interesting fact that Scotland's national poet was a brother of the Craft. His masonic career covered a period of fifteen summers, and from the night in 1781, when he was admitted to a knowledge of the mysteries and privileges of the Square and Compasses, to the day of his death in 1796, he was keenly interested in all that pertained to the brotherhood.

Burns was an enthusiastic Freemason, and more enthusiastic, if less eminent, brethren have not hesitated to assert that he owed all his advancement to the fact that he was a member of "the mystic tie", but these brethren allow their zeal for the Ancient and Honourable Fraternity to outrun their judgement.

Burns had come into his own before the influential Freemasons of the Scottish capital interested themselves in the wonderful "ploughman" who appealed to them as a kind of curiosity; and, for the honour of the Craft, one would not like to think that the Grand Lodge Officers who feasted him for an hour - if they feasted him as a Freemason - then allowed him - as a Freemason - to sink into poverty and distress in old Dumfries.

While it is true that Burns does not owe any of his literary greatness to the fact that he was a Mason, it is, at the same time, noteworthy that almost all his friends in Ayrshire and in Edinburgh were members of the Craft. It is easy to trace a long line of acquaintances, through all the social grades, beginning with Lord Elcho, the Grand Master Mason of Scotland, and finishing with daidlin', drunken Jamie Humphrey, the bletherin' bitch of the Tarbolton Lodge.

Freemasons who like to believe that the rites and ceremonies of the fraternity appealed to the poet and had a share in moulding his mind affirm that in his

> best and most serious writings, in the highest flights of his genius, the spirit of Masonry is ever present, leading, directing, dictating, inspiring;

and in proof of their statement they cite the "Address to the Deil", "Man was made to mourn" and "A man's a man for a' that". It were idle to deny that the beautiful sentiments of the Order had an influence upon the bard, but at the same time there is a strong presumption that Burns was attracted to Freemasonry rather because it was a centre of good-fellowship and social feeling than because it was a system of morality.

(20) Robert Burns as a Freemason, 1921

(21) Robert Burns at Lodge Canongate Kilwinning, 1787

> *Oft, honor'd with supreme command,*
> *Presided o'er the Sons of light.*
>
> from 'The farewell. To the Brethern of
> St James' Lodge, Tarbolton'

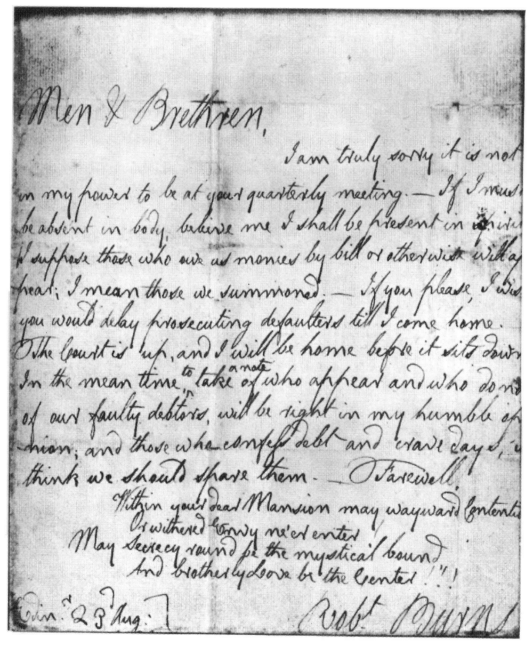

(22) Letter from the poet to the Brethren of St. James's Lodge, Kilwinning, urging delay in prosecuting debtors.

'Now I must reveal to you the chief aim of our order,' he said, 'and if that aim coincides with yours, you may with profit enter our brotherhood. The first and greatest aim and united basis of our order, on which it is established and which no human force can destroy, is the preservation and handing down to posterity of a certain important mystery... that has come down to us from the most ancient times, even from the first man - a mystery upon which, perhaps, the fate of the human race depends. But since this mystery is of such a kind that no one can know it and profit by it if he has not been prepared by a prolonged and diligent self-purification, not every one can hope to attain to it quickly. Hence we have a second aim, which consists in preparing our members, as far as possible reforming their hearts, purifying and enlightening their intelligence by those means which have been revealed to us by tradition from men who have striven to attain this mystery, and thereby to render them fit for the reception of it. Purifying and regenerating our members, we endeavour, thirdly, to improve the whole human race, offering it in our members an example of piety and virtue, and thereby we strive with all our strength to combat the evil that is paramount in the world. Ponder on these things, and I will come again to you,' he said, and went out of the room.

...Half an hour later the rhetor returned to enumerate to the seeker the seven virtues corresponding to the seven steps of the temple of Solomon, in which every freemason must train himself. Those virtues were: (1) discretion, the keeping of the secrets of the order; (2) obedience to the higher authorities of the order; (3) morality; (4) love for mankind; (5) courage; (6) liberality; and (7) love of death.

(23) War and Peace, 1869

> *Within this dear mansion may wayward contention*
> *Or withered envy ne'er enter;*
> *May secresy round be the mystical bound,*
> *And brotherly love be the centre.*
>
> *from 'Ye sons of old Killie'*

Brother Masons...

(24) Lord Glencairn

Lord Glencairn, a man whose worth and brotherly kindness to me I shall remember when time will be no more. -By his interest it is passed in the Caledonian Hunt and entered in their books that they are all to take each a Copy of the second edition, for which they are to pay one guinea.

Letter from Burns to John Ballantine, 1786

(25) Dr Thomas Blacklock, blind poet

It was a letter from Dr Blacklock that persuaded Burns to seek literary fame in Edinburgh

Brother Masons...

(26) William Creech

Publisher of the Edinburgh edition of Burns poems

I have found in Mr Creech, who is my agent forsooth, and Mr Smellie who is to be my printer, that honor and goodness of heart which I always expect in Mr Aiken's friends.

Letter from Burns to Robert Aiken, 1786

(27) William Smellie

Printer of the Edinburgh edition of Burns poems

Adieu! a heart-warm, fond adieu!
  Dear brothers of the mystic tye!
Ye favour'd, ye enlighten'd Few
  Companions of my social joy!
Tho' I to foreign lands must hie,
  Pursuing Fortune's slidd'ry ba,
With melting heart, and brimful eye,
  I'll mind you still, tho' far awa.

May Freedom, Harmony and Love
  Unite you in the grand Design,
Beneath th' Omniscient Eye above,
  The glorious Architect Divine!
That you may keep th' unerring line,
  Still rising by the plummet's law,
Till Order bright, completely shine,
  Shall be my Pray'r when far awa'.

from 'The farewell. To the Brethren of
St James's Lodge, Tarbolton'

(28) Procession of St James's Lodge, Tarbolton

Robert Burns: Reflections of an Age

Women

"But to see her was to love her"

Ladies, after the middle of the century, were altering greatly in habits, taste and dress. By the more easy and frequent intercourse with towns, city modes were passing into every rural mansion. The national plaid was abandoned about 1750 and no longer graced their forms and piquantly hid their features; and in chip hats, toupees, and sacques, they followed the style of Edinburgh, which had been copied from London. Education changed slowly, and they still left school ignorant of geography, history, and grammar, though they spelt more respectably and spoke a little less broadly.

They were deft with their fingers at sewing cambric and plying their tambouring. The old instruments of the mothers or grandmothers, viol and virginal, remained as lumber in the garrets, and they played on the harpsichord and spinet, to which they sang their plaintive Jacobite songs and made their audience weep in sentiment over Prince Charlie. But after the pianoforte was introduced into England in 1767, that instrument took the place of the dear old jingling wires of the spinet. At last spinet and harpsichord were sold at roups for a few shillings to tradesmen and farmers for their daughters to practise on, or to act as sideboards. From the society balls the minuet had gone with the primmer public manners of the past, and reel and country dance had become popular to suit a freer age.

Observers of manners and lovers of the past were noticing and deploring the rise of new and livelier ways. Of old there had been amid woman-kind a dignity and stateliness in deportment, begotten of the severe discipline of the nursery, the rigour of the home, and precision of those gentlewomen of high birth who taught in high flats all feminine accomplishments. If they snuffed it was with formality; if they spoke broad Scots it was without vulgarity; if they said things - and they did say them - that sounded improper to a new generation, their behaviour was a model of propriety, for they had been reared sternly.

By 1780, when these ladies had become frail and wrinkled and old, the austerity of home training, the aloofness of parent and children, so painfully characteristic of former days in Scotland, had passed off, to the regret of many old-fashioned folk. Dr Gregory, an admirable physician, and without doubt an admirable father, spoke of these changes with sorrow: "Every one who can remember a few years back will be sensible of a very striking change in the attention and respect formerly paid by gentlemen to ladies. Their drawing rooms are deserted, and after dinner the gentlemen are impatient till they retire. The behaviour of ladies in the last age was reserved and stately; it would now be considered ridiculously stiff and formal. It certainly had the effect of making them respected." Probably to many today the social ease, whose advent was so lamented, would seem after all stiff as starch and buckrum.

Whether the old days were better than the new may be a matter of doubt. Englishmen found Scots ladies charmingly frank and natural, and more intelligible than their elders, as they gave up broad Scots words and retained only the Scots cadence; but certainly the former school of gentlewomen was far more picturesque and more quaint, more interesting to look at and more entertaining to listen to. They might be poor - they usually were; they might as dowagers live, like Lady Lovat, in a small flat on £140 a year, and be able, like that high born and high-residenced dame, to put only a penny or half-penny in the "brod" on Sabbath when they might go to the fashionable Tron Kirk of Edinburgh; they might go out in pattens and bargain in emphatic vernacular over a fishwife's creel at the "stair foot", and be lighted home with a lantern to the "close mouth" when the tea party was over, to save sixpence for a sedan chair; but in a city and jointure houses in country towns, with their tea and card parties, they wondrously maintained their dignity. They talked of things with blandness on which a reticent age keeps silence; they had read Aphra Behn's plays and spoke freely of *Tom Jones* which the young generation would shut with a slam of disapproval, or hide under the sofa cushion when a visitor came in; they punctuated their caustic sayings with a big pinch of snuff, and sometimes confirmed them with a rattling oath.

(29) Social Life in Scotland in the Eighteenth Century, 1909

For my own part I never had the least thought or inclination of turning Poet till I got once heartily in Love, and then Rhyme and Song were, in a manner, the spontaneous language of my heart.

Common Place Book, 1783-1785

The common every-day dress of the women consisted of coarse blue plaiding petticoats, and a short gown of the same. The married women wore a close mutch, which on Sundays they ornamented with some showy ribbons. Their Sunday dress was composed of linsey-woolsey, which was chiefly spun in the family and given out to be woven. The young unmarried women wore their hair tied round with a ribbon or snood. The plaid, brought over the head, served the purpose of a bonnet.

The ladies and matrons were very particular about their dress. The gowns, which were of silk or brocade patterns, were very long in the waists, with long flowing trains, which were generally tucked up all round. High-heeled shoes with silver buckles were the fashion.

The hair was so dressed as to stand almost erect, and was covered with a fine lawn head-dress with lappets and pinners, which hung down from the back of the head.

About the year 1775 haunch hoops were greatly in vogue among the better classes; and the fashionables wore them round the skirts, of a diameter so great, that before a lady could enter a ball-room she had to raise the one side of her hoop as high as her head, and let the other come in towards her to enable her to pass the doorway.

The lasses in those days, instead of being brought up at the piano, were taught the management of an instrument equally soothing, and generally much more agreeable to the head of the family, namely, the spinning wheel. As the whole of the household linen, as well as blankets, was home-made, a good supply of these articles was a matter of honest pride with the mother and daughters of a family

(30) Tytler's History of Scotland, c1850

O my Luve's like a red, red rose,
  That's newly sprung in June;
O my Luve's like the melodie
  That's sweetly play'd in tune.-

As fair art thou, my bonie lass,
  So deep in luve am I;
And I will love thee still, my Dear,
  Till a' the seas gang dry.-

from 'A red red Rose'

(31) Jean Armour with her granddaughter
Daughter of a master stone mason from Mauchline, she married Burns in 1788

> *Of a' the airts the wind can blaw,*
> *I dearly like the West;*
> *For there the bony Lassie lives,*
> *The Lassie I lo'e best:*
> *There's wild-woods grow, and rivers row,*
> *And mony a hill between;*
> *But day and night my fancy's flight*
> *Is ever wi' my Jean.*
>
> *from 'I love my Jean'*

Women

My Peggy's face, my Peggy's form,
The frost of hermit age might warm;
My Peggy's worth, my Peggy's mind,
Might charm the first of human kind.
I love my Peggy's angel air,
Her face so truly heav'nly fair,
Her native grace so void of art,
But I adore my Peggy's heart.

from 'My Peggy's face'

(32) Margaret Chalmers
Met Burns in Edinburgh at the home of Dr Blacklock

Her looks were like a flow'r in May,
    Her smile was like a simmer morn;
She tripped by the banks of Earn,
    As light's a bird upon a thorn.

Her bonie face it was as meek
    As ony lamb upon a lea;
The evening sun was na'er sae sweet
    As was the blink o' Phemie's e'e.

from 'Blythe was She'

(33) Euphemia Murray
Burns first met 'The Flower of Strathmore' when he visited her uncle, Sir William Murray, of Ochtertyre

> *Fair Empress of the Poet's soul,*
> *And Queen of Poetesses.*
>
> from 'To Clarinda'

(34) Agnes McLehose
Daughter of a Glasgow surgeon, she met Burns at a tea party in Edinburgh. Many letters followed between 'Sylvander' and 'Clarinda'

(35) 'Clarinda's' house, General's Entry

> *I'll ne'er blame my partial fancy,*
> *Naething could resist my Nancy:*
> *But to see her, was to love her;*
> *Love but her, and love for ever.*
>
> from 'Ae fond kiss'

Women

Thy daughters bright thy walks adorn,
  Gay as the gilded summer sky,
Sweet as the dewy, milk-white thorn,
  Dear as the raptured thrill of joy!
Fair Burnet strikes th' adoring eye,
  Heaven's beauties on my fancy shine;
I see the Sire of Love on high,
And own His work indeed divine!

from 'Address to Edinburgh'

(36) Elizabeth Burnet
Daughter of James Burnet, a judge of the Supreme Civil Court of Scotland, she met Burns in Edinburgh

(37) Jessy Lewars
Daughter of the Supervisor of Excise in Dumfries, she helped nurse Burns in the last few months of his life

Or were I in the wildest waste,
  Sae black and bare, sae black and bare,
The desert were a paradise,
  If thou wert there, if thou wert there.
Or were I monarch o' the globe,
  Wi' thee to reign, wi' thee to reign;
The brightest jewel in my crown,
  Wad be my queen, wad be my queen.

from 'Oh wert thou in the cauld blast'

(38) Frances Anna Dunlop
After reading "The Cotter's Saturday Night" she began corresponding with Burns but expressed strong disapproval of his outspoken sympathy with the revolution in France

Mrs Dunlop of Dunlop,
   Dunlop House, Stewarton

Madam - I have written you so often without recg. any answer, that I would not trouble you again but for the circumstances in which I am. An illness which has long hung about me in all probability will speedily send me beyond that bourne whence no traveller returns. Your friendship with which for many years you honoured me was a friendship dearest to my soul. Your conversation and especially your correspondence were at once highly entertaining and instructive. With what pleasure did I use to break up the seal! The remembrance yet adds one pulse more to my poor palpitating heart! - Farewell!!

Letter from Burns to Mrs Dunlop, 1796

Robert Burns: Reflections of an Age

Edinburgh

"Edina! Scotia's darling seat"

Robert Burns: Reflections of an Age

The life of the burghal population of Scotland during the last century, though still simple and primitive, differed considerably from that of the inhabitants of the rural districts. Up till the middle of the century, the city of Edinburgh continued to occupy little more than the space of ground which it had covered two hundred years earlier.

It consisted of a single street, extending along the ridge of the hill from the castle on the west to Holyrood House on the east, together with a large number of narrow alleys or wynds running down the slope on each side of the hill to the Cowgate on the south and the Nor-Loch on the north. In 1752, when the first proposals for the improvement of the city were made, its condition was thus described in a pamphlet written by Sir Gilbert Elliot of Minto, a lord of justiciary. "Placed," he says, "upon the ridge of a hill, Edinburgh admits of but one good street, running from east to west, and even this is tolerably accessible only from one quarter. The narrow lanes leading to the north and south, by reason of their steepness, narrowness, and dirtiness, can only be considered as so many unavoidable nuisances. Many families, no less than ten or a dozen, are obliged to live overhead of each other in the same building; where to all other inconveniences is added that of a common stair, which is no other in effect than an upright street.

It is owing to the same narrowness of situation that the principal street is encumbered with the herb market, the fruit market, and several others. No less observable is the great deficiency of public buildings. If the Parliament House, the churches, and a few hospitals be excepted, what have we to boast of? There is no exchange for our merchants; no repository for our public and private records; no place of meeting for our magistrates and town council; none for the convention of our boroughs, which is entrusted with the inspection of trade. To these and such other reasons it must be imputed, that so few people of rank live in the city; that it is rarely visited by stranger; and that so many local prejudices and narrow notions, inconsistent with polished manners and growing wealth, are still so obstinately retained. To such reasons alone it must be imputed that Edinburgh, which ought to have set the example of industry and improvement, is the last of our trading cities that has shaken off the unaccountable supineness which has so long and so fatally depressed the spirit of the nation."

(39) Tytler's History of Scotland, c1850

(40) Edinburgh Castle in 1779

I had taken the last farewell of my few friends; my chest was on the road to Greenock; I had composed my last song I should ever measure in Caledonia, when a letter from Dr Blacklock to a friend of mine overthrew all my schemes by rousing my poetic ambition, The Doctor belonged to a set of Critics for whose applause I had not even dared to hope. His idea that I would meet with every encouragement for a second edition fired me so much that away I posted to Edinburgh without a single acquaintance in town, or a single letter of introduction in my pocket. The providential care of a good God placed me under the patronage of one of his noblest creatures, the Earl of Glencairn... At Edinburgh I was in a new world...

Letter from Burns to Dr John Moore, 1787

(41) Professor Dugald Stewart

(42) Henry Mckenzie

I have been introduced to a good many of the noblesse, but my avowed Patrons and Patronesses are, the Duchess of Gordon - the Countess of Glencairn, with my lord and lady Betty - the Dean of Faculty - Sir John Whiteford. I have likewise warm friends among the Literati, Professors Stewart, Blair, Greenfield, and Mr McKenzie the Man of feeling. Dugald Stewart and some of my learned friends have put me in the periodical paper called the Lounger...

Letter from Burns to John Ballantine, 1786

I am in a fair way of becoming as eminent as Thomas a Kempis or John Bunyan; and you may expect henceforth to see my birthday inserted among the wonderful events...

Letter from Burns to Gavin Hamilton, 1786

(43) Burns at a literary gathering

(44) His behaviour was suitable to his appearance: neither awkward, arrogant, nor affected, but decent, dignified and simple. In the midst of a large company of ladies and gentlemen assembled to see him, and attentive to his every look, word, and motion, he was no way disconcerted, but seemed perfectly easy, unembarrassed, and unassuming.

Letter from Robert Anderson to James Currie, 1799

> *Edina! Scotia's darling seat!*
> *All hail thy palaces and tow'rs,*
> *Where once beneath a Monarch's feet*
> *Sat Legislation's sov'reign pow'rs!*
> *From marking wildly-scatt'red flow'rs,*
> *As on the banks of Ayr I stray'd,*
> *And singing, lone, the ling'ring hours,*
> *I shelter in thy honor'd shade.*
>
> *from 'Address to Edinburgh'*

Edinburgh

By 1770 there were signs setting in of the approaching transformation of Edinburgh - in the city and society. It was full time, for the crowd of inhabitants was now denser, and the streets and wynds were as malodorous as ever. One night arm-in-arm Boswell and Dr. Johnson marched slowly up the High Street, inhaling the 'evening effluvia'. Then the great man grumbled into the ear of his friend, "Sir, I can smell you in the dark!" The town which had remained within its ancient bounds and walls for 250 years, was becoming too circumscribed for its population, which filled the streets that had grown in height instead of length; spaces behind the Canongate and High Street, once occupied by pleasant gardens, had long been built over by wynds and courts, and no more room was left for its increasing inhabitants to build on. About 1760 there had been erected squares of 'self-contained' houses south of the town, to which some richer familes resorted; and yet, though only a few minutes, walk from their business and their friends, Brown Square and George Square were considered terribly out of the way, so that gentlemen required to take refreshment in the tavern before the journey. In 1772 the North Bridge was finished, and access to a new district became easier, while old merchants spoke with astonishment about the enormous rents of £30 or £40 which ambitious rivals were paying for shops beside the "Brig". Plans by that time had been formed for streets on the other side of the 'Nor' Loch' (the lake of swamp now the Princes Street Gardens); but slow progress was made till 1780, when new streets were springing up, and houses in Princes Street, George Street, and Queen Street were advancing westward. From the old flats descended in gradual exodus persons of position and quality, who, instead of a modest rental of £15 or £20, were able now, through advancing wealth and larger incomes, to pay £100 for mansions which contrasted strangely with the mean and dirty abodes from which they emerged. They left those dwellings where there had been little cleanliness or comfort, where fetid air brought sickness and death to their lives, where infectious diseases passed like wildfire through the inmates of a crowded common stair, bringing havoc to many a household.

Town and town-life underwent a revolution, and many a quaintly pleasant and picturesque feature of Scottish society soon became a mere memory.

Fortunately, the old taverns lost their "genteel" company, and gentlemen met temperately at home in their spacious dining-rooms, instead of in miserable cellars, over their mutchkin and glass.

The sedan-chairs were becoming worn out, like the chairmen who carried in them so many occupants, with towering powdered headdresses, to the dance, and for 6d. an hour had shaken their burdens over the causeway, and up closes where no carriage could enter. These were being discarded for hackney coaches that drove swiftly along handsome though unfinished streets; but for many a year some ladies of the olden type still were borne along to their tea parties in the venerable chairs of their grandmothers. Other changes came, some that were not grateful. The delightful old simplicity of manners, the unceremonious friendliness, the genial gatherings around, the tea-table, where the company discussed their "fifty friends within five hundred yards", the familiar intercourse and sympathy between rich and poor, formed by proximity in the same turnpike stair; the quaint old dowager ladies of rank and poverty, who, on "small genteel incomes," and with one maid-servant gave slender entertainments in a fourth flat, all these passed away for ever.

By the close of the century these "lands," in multitudinous closes, were becoming deserted by the upper classes. Although some clung on tenaciously to their patrimonial tenements, the bulk of quality and fashion had gone to reside on the other side of the swampy North Loch, quitting for ever the old haunts where so long a teeming friendly population of gentle and simple had dwelt, leaving for ever ancient flats associated with ages of dirt and dignity, of smells and social mirth. The old rooms received new occupants; pawnbrokers lived where lords of session had dwelt; washer women cleaned clothes in chambers where fine ladies had worn them; mechanics, with their squalling brats, occupied apartments whose decorated mantelpieces and painted ceiling told of departed greatness, rooms where in bygone days the gayest of the town had met when they were scenes of all that had been brightest and merriest of olden life.

With the New Town of Edinburgh began a new social existence in Scotland.

(45) Social Life in Scotland in the Eighteenth Century, 1909

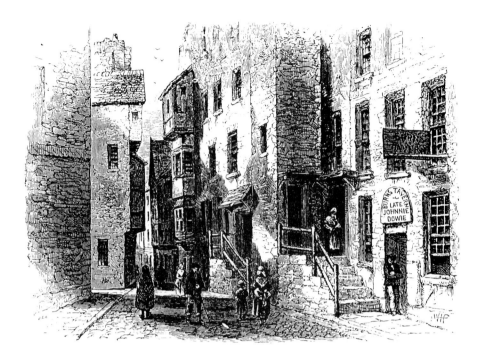

(46) Buildings at the foot of Libberton's Wynd, Cowgate, demolished to make way for George IV Bridge. Burns spent many happy social hours in Johnnie Dowie's Tavern during his stay in Edinburgh.

(47) Edinburgh Lawnmarket. It was here, in Baxter's Close, that Burns took up lodging on his first visit to the Capital, sharing a room with John Richmond, an old Mauchline friend.

DEDICATION

TO THE

SECOND, OR EDINBURGH, EDITION.

OF

THE POEMS OF BURNS.

TO THE

NOBLEMEN AND GENTLEMEN

OF

THE CALEDONIAN HUNT.

My Lords and Gentlemen:

A Scottish Bard, proud of the name, and whose highest ambition is to sing in his country's service—where shall he so properly look for patronage as to the illustrious names of his native land; those who bear the honours and inherit the virtues of their ancestors? The Poetic Genius of my Country found me, as the prophetic bard Elijah did Elisha—at the plough; and threw her inspiring mantle over me. She bade me sing the loves, the joys, the rural scenes and rural pleasures of my native soil, in my native tongue: I tuned my wild, artless notes, as she inspired. She whispered me to come to this ancient Metropolis of Caledonia, and lay my Songs under your honoured protection: I now obey her dictates.

Though much indebted to your goodness, I do not approach you, my Lords and Gentlemen, in the usual style of dedication, to thank you for past favours: that path is so hackneyed by prostituted learning, that honest rusticity is ashamed of it. Nor do I present this Address with the venal soul of a servile author, looking for a continuation of those favours: I was bred to the plough, and am independent. I come to claim the common Scottish name with you, my illustrious Countrymen; and to tell the world that I glory in the title. I come to congratulate my country, that the blood of her ancient heroes still runs uncontaminated; and that from your courage, knowledge, and public spirit, she may expect protection, wealth, and liberty. In the last place, I come to proffer my warmest wishes to the Great Fountain of Honour, the Monarch of the Universe, for your welfare and happiness.

When you go forth to waken the echoes, in the ancient and favourite amusement of your forefathers, may Pleasure ever be of your party: and may social Joy await your return! When harassed in courts or camps with the jostlings of bad men and bad measures, may the honest consciousness of injured worth attend your return to your native seats; and may domestic happiness, with a smiling welcome, meet you at your gates! May corruption shrink at your kindling indignant glance; and may tyranny in the ruler, and licentiousness in the people, equally find you an inexorable foe!

I have the honour to be,
With the sincerest gratitude and highest respect,
My Lords and Gentlemen,
Your most devoted humble Servant,
ROBERT BURNS.

Edinburgh,
April 4, 1787.

(48) Dedication to the Edinburgh edition

Never did Saul's armour sit so heavy on David when going to encounter Goliah, as does the encumbering robe of public notice with which the friendship and patronage of some "names dear to fame" have invested in me. I do not say this in the ridiculous idea of seeming self-abasement, and affected modesty. I have long studied myself, and I think I know pretty exactly what ground I occupy, both as man and as a poet; and however the world, or a friend, may sometimes differ from me in that particular, I stand for it, in silent resolve with all the tenaciousness of Property. I am willing to believe that my abilities deserved a better fate than the veriest shades of life; but to be dragged forth, with all my imperfections on my head, to the full glare of learned and polite observation, is what, I am afraid, I shall have bitter reason to repent.

I mention this to you, once for all, merely, in the Confessor style, to disburthen my conscience, and that, "When proud Fortune's ebbing tide recedes" - you may bear me witness, when my buble of fame was at the highest, I stood, unintoxicated, with rueful resolve, to the hastening time when the stroke of envious Calumny, with all the eagerness of vengeful triumph should dash it to the ground.

Letter from Burns to William Greenfield, 1786

(49)　The Royal Mile, Edinburgh

Robert Burns: Reflections of an Age

Excise

"I'm turn'd a Gauger"

Robert Burns: Reflections of an Age

In the year 1725 contraband trading received an unforeseen impetus from the imposition of 6d per bushel on malt, which gathering strength, eventually increased the practice to an enormous extent. "Twopenny ale", home-brewed mostly, so-called from the fact that a Scotch pint could be purchased for twopence, was then the universal drink of the country. The imposition of this tax was received by the populace as personal, and deeply resented, and although it was reduced to 3d per bushel, the tax gave such universal offence that brewing of this harmless and wholesome ale, gradually yet steadily declined, to give place to the introduction of the more harmful potency of smuggled spirits. In the further development of the "free-trade" a crisis may be said to have been reached, when following the American War of Independence and the war with France, which broke out in 1792, the British Government was compelled to increase the taxation to a height never before reached. In a like degree the contraband trade increased and developed. The spirit of retaliation was more than general, and high and low, old and young, all alike combined in the support of the "fair-trade", and made it their business to cooperate in concealing and transporting the "goods", as well as outwitting and "jinking the gauger".

Two branches of the preventative service existed, such as it was, represented by the Customs and Excise officers for the shore, and the Revenue cutters for the patrol of the seas, but both were inadequate and defective. The officers of Customs and Excisemen were all too few for the work; moreover their opposition was often very doubtful and half-hearted, and certainly without the cooperation of the military they scarcely dared to venture on assuming the offensive.

The Revenue cutters in 1794 were *The Royal Charlotte* and *Royal George* of sixty men each, and the *Prince of Wales* and *Princess Elizabeth* of fifty men each. Other small cutters and sloops were the *Royal George, Prince of Wales, Prince William Henry, Princess Royal, Prince Edward, Prince Ernest Augustus* and *Osnaburgh*.

But the speed and smartness of these vessels were not all in accordance with the royalty of their names. The smugglers built speedy craft that easily outsailed them, and it was not uncommon for a derisive smuggler, secure in the knowledge of his better sailing qualities, to run close to the King's craft and jeeringly hold out a tow-rope.

(50) Smuggling in the Solway, 1908

You know, I daresay, of an application I lately made to your Board, to be admitted an Officer of Excise. I have, according to form, been examined by a Supervisor and today I give in his Certificate with a request for an Order for instructions, In this affair, if I succeed, I am afraid I shall but too much need a patronising Friend. Propriety of conduct as a Man, and fidelity and attention as an Officer, I dare engage for; but with anything like business, I am totally unacquainted. The man who till within these eighteen months was never the wealthy master of ten guineas, can be but ill-acquainted with the busy routine. I had intended to have closed my late meteorous appearance on the stage of Life, in the country Farmer; but after discharging some filial and fraternal claims, I find I could only fight for existence in that miserable manner, which I have lived to see repeatedly throw a venerable Parent in the jaws of a Jail; where, but for the Poor Man's last and often best friend, Death, he might have ended his days.

I know, Sir, that to need your goodness is to have a claim on it: may I therefore beg your Patronage to forward me in this affair till I be appointed to a Division; where, by the help of rigid Economy, I shall try to support that Independance so dear to my soul, but which has too often been so distant from my situation.

Letter from Burns to Robert Graham of Fintry, 1788

Excise

Excise - a hateful tax levied upon commodities and adjudged not by the common judges of property but by wretches hired by those to whom the excise is paid.

(51) Dr Johnson's Dictionary, 1755

At this period the people groaned under an intolerable burden of hateful imposts. Excise duties were levied on all luxuries and on most of the necessaries of life, comprising such articles as salt, tea, coffee, soap, starch, candles, paper, hides, skins, printed goods, glass, bricks, and of course, on beer, spirits, wine and tobacco. Smuggling was rampant. Beer was illegally brewed and spirits illicitly distilled all over Scotland. Almost the entire population sympathised with or connived at, the evasion of the Revenue Laws, which were necessarily severe and constantly exercised.

Ruinous penalties were imposed, lengthy periods of imprisonment were inflicted, and unlucky smugglers were occasionally hanged for having killed an Excise or Customs Officer in some desperate encounter. As a natural consequence of this state of things, the Revenue officers of the period were unpopular, for they were the visible embodiment of obnoxious and oppressive fiscal laws and regulations.

(52) Burns: Excise Officer and Poet, 1898

But what d'ye think, my trusty Fier,
I'm turn'd a Gauger - Peace be here!
Parnassian Quines I fear, I fear,
Ye'll now disdain me,
And then my fifty pounds a year
Will little gain me.

from 'Epistle to Dr Blacklock'

My Excise Commission ... I regard as my sheet anchor in life.

Letter from Burns to Robert Graham, 1788

43

It was in this year that the great smuggling trade corrupted all the west coast, especially the laigh lands about the Troon and the Loans. The tea was going like the chaff, the brandy like well-water, and the wastrie of all things was terrible. There was nothing minded but the riding of cadgers by day, and excisemen by night - and battles between the smugglers and the king's men, both by sea and land. There was a continual drunkenness and debauchery; and our session, that was but on the lip of this whirlpool of iniquity, had an awful time o't. I did all that was in the power of nature to keep my people from the contagion: I preached sixteen times from the text, "Render to Caesar the things that are Caesar's." I visited, and I exhorted; I warned, and I prophesied; I told them that, although the money came in like sclate stones, it would go like the snow off the dyke. But for all I could do, the evil got in among us, and we had no less than three contested bastard bairns upon our hands at one time, which was a thing never heard of in a parish of the shire of Ayr since the Reformation.

Shortly after the revival of the smuggling, an exciseman was put among us, and the first was Robin Bicker, a very civil lad that had been a flunkey with Sir Hugh Montgomerie, when he was a residenter in Edinburgh, before the old Sir Hugh's death. He was a queer fellow, and had a coothy way of getting in about folk, the which was very serviceable to him in his vocation; nor was he overly gleg; but when a job was ill done, and he was obliged to notice it, he would often break out on the smugglers for being so stupid; so that for an exciseman he was wonderful well liked, and did not object to a waught of brandy at a time, when the auld wives ca'd it well-water. It happened, however, that some unneighbourly person sent him notice of a clecking of tea chests, or brandy kegs, at which both Jenny and Betty Pawkie were the howdies. Robin could not but therefore enter the house; however, before going in, he just cried at the door to somebody on the road, so as to let the twa industrious lasses hear he was at hand. They were not slack in closing the trance-door, and putting stoups and stools behind it, so as to cause trouble, and give time before anybody could bet in. They then emptied their chaff-bed, and filled the tikeing with tea, and Betty went in on the top, covering herself with blanket, and graining like a woman in labour.

(53) Annals of the Parish, Years 1761 and 1778

> *Searching auld wives' barrels,*
>   *Ochon, the day!*
> *That clarty barm should stain my laurels;*
>   *But- what'll ye say!*
> *These murvin things ca'd wives and weans*
> *Wad muve the very hearts o' stanes!*
>
> *'An Extemporaneous Effusion on being appointed to the Excise'*

I mentioned to you my Excise hopes and views. I have been once more a lucky fellow in that quarter. The Excisemen's Salaries are now £50 per Ann. and I believe the Board have been so oblidging as fix me in the Division in which I live; and I suppose I shall begin doing duty at the commencement of next month.

Five days in the week, or four at least, I must be on horseback, and very frequently ride thirty or forty miles ere I return; besides four different kinds of book-keeping to post every day.

Letters from Burns to Mrs Dunlop, 1789

a Carefull offr	Andw Brodie	32	8	1
a carefull good offr	John Burnet	38	9	2
a good offr	James Booth	37	9	4
The Poet, does pretty well	Robert Burns	32	3	7
a good offr	Wm Brown	28	5	3
	John Black	33	6	3
a good offr	Robt Barclay	41	12	

(54) Facsimile of portion of page of "Character Book" of the Scottish Excise Board, 1792

People may talk as they please of the ignominy of the Excise, but what will support my family and keep me independant of the world is to me a very important matter; and I had much rather that my Profession borrowed credit from me, than that I borrowed credit from my Profession.

Letter from Burns to Lady Elizabeth Cunninghame, 1789

I am happy to inform you I have just got an appointment to the first or Port Division as it is called, which adds twenty pounds per annum more to my Salary. My excise income is now cash paid, seventy pounds a year; and this I hold until I am appointed supervisor. So much for my usual good luck. My perquisities I hope to make worth £15 or £20 more. So Rejoice with them that do Rejoice.

Letter from Burns to Maria Riddell, 1792

(55) Portion of Excise Book kept by Burns

> *Ye men of wit and wealth, why all this sneering*
> *'Gainst poor Excisemen? give the cause a hearing:*
> *What are your landlords' rent-rolls? taxing ledgers:*
>   *What premiers, what? even Monarchs' mighty gaigers:*
> *Nay, what are priests? those seeming godly wisemen:*
>   *What are they, pray? but spiritual Excisemen.*
>
> 'Lines written on a window, at the King's Arms Tavern, Dumfries'

ANNO REGNI VICESIMO SEPTIMO Cap. 57.

WHEREAS, by an Act passed in the Third Year of the Reign of King George the First, a Duty of Two Pennies Scots, or One Sixth Part of a Penny Sterling, over and above the Duties of Excise paid or payable to His Majesty, His Heirs and Successors, was granted and made payable to the Magistrates and Town Council of the Town of Dumfries, for the Use of the Community thereof, upon every Scots Pint of Ale and Beer that should be either brewed, brought in, or vended, tapped, or sold within the said Town, and Privileges thereof, for the Term of Nineteen Years, and to the End of the then next Session of Parliament, to be applied to the Uses therein mentioned: And whereas, by an Act passed in the Tenth Year of the Reign of His late Majesty King George the Second, the said Duty was continued and made payable to the said Magistrates and Town Council, from the Expiration of the said former Act, for the Term of Twenty-five Years, and to the End of the then next Session of Parliament; and by the said last recited Act, there was also granted to the said Magistrates and Council, for the same Term, certain other Duties on all Goods, Wares, Merchandises, and other Commodities, imported or exported into or out of the Port of the said Town, and on the Tonnage of all Shipping arriving in the said Port, to be applied and accounted for in Manner therein mentioned, videlicet; for every Ton of Goods, Wares, or Merchandises, which should be imported into the said Port (except Coals, Lime, and Lime-stone), the Sum of Eight-pence Sterling, and so in Proportion for any larger or smaller Quantity; for every Ton of Goods, Wares, or Merchandises, which should be loaded or shipped off, or exported from the said Port, the Sum of Eight-pence Sterling,

(56) Extract from Amendment Act, 1787

Robert Burns: Reflections of an Age

When the smuggling French brig Rosamond, ran aground in the Solway Firth, in February 1792, Lewars, who had been despatched to Dumfries for a guard of dragoons, was long in returning, and one of the officers, becoming impatient, said:- "I wish the deil had him for his pains; write a song about him, Burns". The Poet moved off a little distance, strode about for a short time, and returning, chanted to his delighted companions:- 'The deil cam fiddlin' through the town an' danced awa wi' the exciseman'.

Lewars returned shortly afterwards with his dragoons; Burns at once placed himself at the head of this small party, waded sword in hand to the brig, and was the first man to board. The vessel was condemned, and sold next day, with all her arms and stores, at Dumfries. Burns purchased four of her rusty carronades for £3, and, moved by some quixotic impulse, or humorous fancy, it is said he sent them to the French Legislative Assembly, with a letter requesting them "to accept them as a present, and a mark of admiration and sympathy".

It is said they were seized by the Customs at Dover.

(57) Burns: Excise Officer and Poet, 1898

> *The deil cam fiddlin thro' the town,*
> *And danc'd awa wi' the' Exciseman;*
> *And ilka wife cries, auld Mahoun,*
> *I wish you luck o' the prize, man.*
>
> *from 'The de'ils awa wi' the' Exciseman'*

I have been appointed to act in the capacity of Supervisor here... This appointment is only temporary, & during the illness of the present incumbent; but I look forward to an early period when I shall be appointed in full form: a consumation devoutly to be wished.

Letter from Burns to Mrs Dunlop, 1794

Robert Burns: Reflections of an Age
Revolution

"Liberty's a glorious feast"

Rara temporum felicitas, ubi sentire, quæ velis; & quæ sentias, dicere licet
TACIT

My Lord BACON and some late philosophers in England have begun to put the science of man on a new footing, and have engaged the attention, and excited the curiosity of the public. So true it is, that however other nations may rival us in poetry, and excel us in some other agreeable arts, the improvements in reason and philosophy can only be owing to a land of toleration and of liberty.

(58) A Treatise of Human Nature, 1739

Man is born free; and everywhere he is in chains.

(59) The Social Contract and Discourses, 1762

But of real literature, save the poems of Ramsay, there were still few signs; till in 1738, there appeared in London a *Treatise of Human Nature* by David Hume, then twenty five years old. It fell as the author cheerfully confesses, "stillborn from the press"; which did not discourage him from publishing, within a few years, those philosophical essays which slowly established his name in literature and his place in sceptical philosophy, creating a panic fright in orthodox circles, which was borne with placidity by the simple-souled and good-humoured philosopher - verily, the "mildest-mannered man that ever scuttled" a creed.

After the middle of the century there was a wider awakening of intellectual life in Edinburgh, and in Scotland generally. Adam Fergusson, Hugh Blair, Adam Smith, and others, were soon to make Edinburgh a literary centre and literature a matter of fashion to gentlemen.

Intellectual activity was spreading in all circles. The Select Society, founded by the versatile and energetic Allan Ramsay, changed in 1755 to the Society of Encouraging Art, Science and Industry. Noblemen, lairds, judges, ministers, advocates engaged in these meetings.

(60)   Social Life in Scotland in the Eighteenth Century, 1909

I could not have given any mere man credit for half the intelligence Mr [Adam] Smith discovers in his book. I would covet much to have his ideas respecting the present state of some quarters of the world that are or have been the scenes of considerable revolutions since his book was written.

Letter from Burns to Robert Graham, 1789

Revolution

It becomes a man of sense to think for himself...
Letter from Burns to Robert Muir, 1788

Have not I, to me, a more prescious stake in my Country's welfare, than the richest Dukedom in it? I have a large family of children, and the probability of more. I have three sons, whom, I see already, have brought with them into the world souls ill qualified to inhabit the bodies of Slaves. Can I look tamely on, and see any machination to wrest from them, the birthright of my boys, the little independant Britons in whose veins runs my own blood? No! I will not! - should my heart stream around my attempt to defend it!

Does any man tell me, that my feeble efforts can be of no service; and that it does not belong to my humble station to meddle with the concerns of a People? I tell him, that it is on such individuals as I, that for the hand of support and the eye of intelligence, a Nation has to rest. The uninformed mob may swell a Nation's bulk; and the titled, tinsel Courtly throng may be its feathered ornament, but the number of those who are elevated enough in life, to reason and reflect; and yet low enough to keep clear of the venal contagion of a Court; these are a Nation's strength.

Letter from Burns to John Erskine, 1793

*Here's a health to them that's awa,
Here's a health to them that's awa;
Here's a health to Charlie, the chief o' the clan,
Altho' that his band be sma'.
May Liberty meet wi' success!
May Prudence protect her frae evil!
May Tyrants and Tyranny tine i' the mist,
And wander their way to the devil!*

from 'Here's a health to them that's awa'

> *When Guilford good our Pilot stood,*
> *An' did our hellim thraw, man*
> *Ae night, at tea, began a plea,*
> *Within America, man:*
> *Then up they gat the maskin-pat,*
> *And in the sea did jaw, man;*
> *An' did nae less, in full Congress,*
> *Than quite refuse our law, man.*
>
> *from 'A fragment'*

AMERICAN DECLARATION OF INDEPENDENCE - 1776

We hold these truths to be self evident, that all men are created equal, that they are endowed by their Creator with certain unalienable rights, that among these are life, liberty and the pursuit of happiness. That, to secure these rights, governments are instituted among men, deriving their just powers from the consent of the governed. That, whenever any form of government becomes destructive of these ends, it is the right of the people to alter or to abolish it, and to institute new government, laying its foundation on such principles, and organising its powers in such form, as to them shall seem most likely to effect their safety and happiness.

Prudence, indeed, will dictate that governments long established should not be changed for light and transient causes; and accordingly, all experience has shown, that mankind are more disposed to suffer, while evils are sufferable, than to right themselves by abolishing the forms to which they are accustomed.

But, when a long train of abuses and usurpations, pursuing invariably the same object, evinces a design to reduce them under absolute despotism, it is their right, it is their duty, to throw off such government, and to provide new guards for the future security.

> *No Spartan tube, no Attic shell,*
> *No lyre Eolian I awake;*
> *'Tis Liberty's bold note I swell,*
> *Thy harp, Columbia, let me take.*
> *See gathering thousands, while I sing,*
> *A broken chain, exulting, bring,*
> *And dash it in a tyrant's face!*
> *And dare him to his very beard,*
> *And tell him, he no more is feared,*
> *No more the Despot of Columbia's race.*
> *A tyrant's proudest insults braved,*
> *They shout, a People freed! They hail an Empire saved.*
>
> *from 'Ode for General Washington's birthday'*

REVOLUTION IN FRANCE

Tuesday, July 14. This day was pregnant with great events; early in the morning the Hotel de Ville ordered the cockades to be changed for pink, white, and blue. A remark made by several of the militia, that Count d'Artois' livery was turned up with green, was the cause of this change. Before I enter any farther on this day's exploits, I must premise that every man, of every rank, wore a cockade; the militia therefore was soon confounded and mixed with the rest of the inhabitants. Between ten and eleven about a thousand stout men, some with, others without arms, went towards the Invalids, on the skirts of Paris, West, and not half a quarter of a mile distant from the Ecole Militaire, on the plains of which the troops are encamped. The one thousand men increased to two or three thousand in going along, incessantly crying out, *Vive le Tiers Etat* (Long live the Third Class.) This body not certainly very formidable for the place of the Invalids, that mounted 22 pieces of cannon, and was so near the camp, demanded admittance sword-in-hand, threatening to burst open the iron-gates if it was not complied with. The Governor after a short conference with his officers opened the gates, and let the people enter. Forthwith all the cannon were secured, and carried away by the horses they had brought with them, and then the people proceeded to the armory. There they found new muskets to the number of 20,000. I cannot describe to you the joy that sparkled in every young man's countenance as he seized his piece. Thus armed, they went in triumph Eastward, to the Battille, the mansion of sorrow, where so many have been confined by the hand of despotism. Opposite to it they levelled their battery, and began to fire. The ditches that surround the fortress were soon filled with pieces of wood, chairs, stones, &c. and no doubt, some brave fellows would have attempted the escalade, had not the Governor, M. de Launay, hung out a white flag, and let down the draw-bridge. In an instant two or three hundred more entered; when De Launay ordered his soldiers to draw up the bridge, and to fall on the people, who had so unwarily fallen into his snare

(61)   Dumfries Weekly Journal, 1789

As to France, I was her enthusiastic votary in the beginning of the business. - When she came to shew her old avidity for conquest, in annexing Savoy, & c to her dominions, & invading the rights of Holland, I altered my sentiments.

Letter from Burns to Robert Graham of Fintry, 1793

Robert Burns: Reflections of an Age

> *If I'm design'd yon lordling's slave-*
> *By Nature's law design'd-*
> *Why was an independent wish,*
> *E'er planted in my mind?*
>
> from 'Man was made to mourn'

It has been said, it seems, that I not only belong to, but head a disaffected party in this place. I know of no party in this place, either Republican or Reform, except an old party of Burgh-Reform; with which I never had anything to do. Individuals, both Republican & Reform, we have, though not many of either; but if they have associated, it is more than I have the least knowledge of: & if there exists such an association, it must consist of such obscure, nameless beings, as precludes any possibility of my being known to them, or they to me.

I was in the playhouse one night, when Ça ira was called for. I was in the middle of the pit, and from the pit the clamour arose. One or two individuals with whom I occasionally associate were of the party, but I neither knew of the Plot, nor joined in the Plot; nor ever opened my lips to hiss, or huzza, that, or any other Political tune whatever. I looked on myself as far too obscure a man to have any weight in quelling a Riot; at the same time, as a character of higher respectability, than to yell in the howlings of a rabble.

I never uttered any invectives against the King. His private worth, it is altogether impossible that such a man as I, can appreciate; and in his Public capacity, I always revered, & ever will, with the soundest loyalty, revere, the Monarch of Great Britain, as, to speak in Masonic, the sacred Keystone of our Royal Arch Constitution.

As to Reform principles, I look upon the British Constitution, as settled at the Revolution, to be the most glorious on earth, or that perhaps the wit of man can frame; at the same time, I think, & you know what High and distinguished Characters have for some time thought so, that we have a good deal deviated from the original principles of that Constitution; particularly, that an alarming system of corruption has pervaded the connection between the executive power and the House of Commons. This is the truth, the whole truth, of my Reform opinions; opinions which, before I was aware of the complection of these innovating times, I too unguardedly sported with: but henceforth, I seal my lips.

Letter from Burns to Robert Graham of Fintry, 1793

DUMFRIES, February 17.

It is with pleasure we hear, that his Majesty has been graciously pleased to accept of the offer of the Gentlmen of this place to form themselves into two companies of Volunteers, for the defence of the town and neighbourhood.

(62) Dumfries Weekly Journal, 1795

Does haughty Gaul invasion threat,
  Then let the louns bewaure, Sir,
There's Wooden Walls upon our seas,
  And Volunteers on shore, Sir:
The Nith shall run to Corsincon,
  And Criffell sink in Solway,
E'er we permit a Foreign Foe
  On British ground to rally

O, let us not, like snarling tykes,
  In wrangling be divided,
Till, slap! come in an unco loun,
  And wi' a rung decide it!
Be Britain still to Britain true,
  Amang oursels united;
For never but by British hands
  Must British wrongs be righted.

The kettle o' the Kirk and State,
  Perhaps a clout may fail in't;
But deil a foreign tinkler-loun
  Shall ever ca' a nail in't:
Our fathers' Blude the kettle bought,
  And wha wad dare to spoil it,
By Heavens, the sacreligious dog
  Shall fuel be to boil it!

The wretch that would a Tyrant own,
  And the wretch, his true-sworn brother,
Who'd set the Mob above the Throne,
  May they be damn'd together!
Who will not sing, God save the King,
  Shall hang as high's the steeple;
But while we sing, God save the King,
  We'll ne'er forget The People!

'The Dumfries Volunteers'

The Rights of Man
Thomas Paine

The French Constitution says, There shall be no titles; and of consequence, all that class of equivocal generation which in some countries is called 'aristocracy' and in others 'nobility', is done away with, and the peer is exalted into MAN.

Titles are but nicknames, and every nickname is a title. The thing is perfectly harmless in itself, but it marks a sort of foppery in the human character, which degrades it.

For what we can forsee, all Europe may form but one great Republic, and man be free of the whole.

(63) The Rights of Man, 1791

(64)

Ye see yon birkie ca'd, a lord,
  Wha struts, and stares, and a' that,
Though hundreds worship at his word,
  He's but a coof for a' that.
For a' that, and a' that,
  His ribband, star and a' that,
The man of independant mind,
He looks and laughs at a' that.

from 'For a' that and a' that'

Then let us pray that come it may,
  As come it will for a' that,
That Sense and Worth, o'er a' the earth
  Shall bear the gree, and a' that.
For a' that, and a' that,
  Its coming yet for a' that,
That Man to Man the warld o'er,
Shall brothers be for a' that.

from 'For a' that and a' that'

Robert Burns: Reflections of an Age

Dumfries

"How lovely Nith, thy fruitful vales"

Character and Manners.—The town of Dumfries serving in some measure as a capital, not merely to this shire, but also to Galloway, and having such easy and regular intercourse with London, with Edinburgh, and even with the capital of Ireland, has thus become remarkable as a provincial town for elegance, information, and varied amusement. The gentry from the neighbouring country, are thence often inclined, either to prefer it as a place of residence, or to pay it occasional visits. Its establishments for education hold out considerable inducements to persons of moderate fortune, who may wish their children to enjoy the advantages of a well-conducted public education, without being removed from under their own immediate inspection. The character of the inhabitants, is allowed to be, in general, very respectable. They are charitable and benevolent, hospitable to strangers, and mix frequently amongst themselves in domestic intercourse. In their disposition and manners they are social and polite; and the town, together with the neighbourhood a few miles around it, furnishes a society, amongst whom a person of a moderate fortune may spend his days, with as much satisfaction and enjoyment, as, perhaps, in any part of these kingdoms.

(65) Dumfries Parish
First Statistical Account, 1790s

(66) View of the Nith, Dumfries.

Some years ago your good Town did me the honor of making me an Honorary Burgess. Will your Honors allow me to request that this mark of distinction may extend so far, as to put me on the footing of a real Freeman of the Town, in the Schools?

Letter from Burns to The Lord Provost, Baillies and Town Council of Dumfries, 1793

(67) View of Dumfries

In the spring of 1796 the burgh once again suffered from a dearth of food, and consequent disturbances... the lower classes...suffering the pains of a protracted scarcity, rose to riot and pillage... The alarming saturnalia began on Saturday, 12th March, 1796, became increasingly violent on Sabbath, 13th, and were with difficulty suppressed in the evening of the latter day.

(68) History of the Burgh of Dumfries, 1867

I know not how you are in Ayrshire, but here, we have actual famine, and that too in the midst of plenty. Many days my family, and hundreds of other families, are absolutely without one grain of meal; as money cannot purchase it. How long the Swinish Multitude will be quiet, I cannot tell: they threaten daily.

Letter from Burns to Mrs Dunlop, 1796

> No more of your guests, be they titled or not,
> And cookery the first in the nation,
> Who is proof to thy personal converse and wit'
> Is proof to all other temptation
>
> *'To John Syme'*

(69) John Syme, Distributer of Stamps for Dumfriesshire, accompanied Burns on his Galloway tour in 1794 and was also a member of the Dumfries Volunteers.

> Here's, a bottle and an honest friend!
> What wad ye wish for mair, man?
>
> *from 'Here's, a bottle and an honest friend'*

(70) The Globe Inn, Dumfries

TO SIR JOHN SINCLAIR,
    OF ULBSTER.
        ELLISLAND, 1791

Sir,

The following circumstance has, I believe, been omitted in the statistical account transmitted to you of the parish of Dunscore, in Nithsdale. I beg leave to send it to you, because it is new, and may be useful. How far it is deserving of a place in your patriotic publication, you are the best judge.

To store the minds of the lower classes with useful knowledge is certainly of very great importance, both to them as individuals, and to society at large. Giving them a turn for reading and reflection is giving them a source of innocent and laudable amusement, and, besides, raises them to a more dignified degree in the scale of rationality. Impressed with this idea, a gentleman in this parish, Robert Riddell, Esq. of Glenriddell, set on foot a species of circulating library, on a plan so simple as to be practicable in any corner of the country; and so useful, as to deserve the notice of every country gentleman who thinks the improvement of that part of his own species whom chance has thrown into the humble walks of the peasant and artizan a matter worthy of his attention.

Mr. Riddell got a number of his own tenants and farming neighbours to form themselves into a society for the purpose of having a library among themselves. They entered into a legal engagement to abide by it for three years; with a saving clause of two, in case of a removal to distance, or death. Each member, at his entry, paid five shillings; and at each of their meetings, which were held every fourth Saturday, sixpence more. With their entry-money, and the credit which they took on the faith of their future funds, they laid in a tolerable stock of books at the commencement. What authors they were to purchase was always decided by the majority. At every meeting all the books, under certain fines and forfeitures, by way of penalty, were to be produced; and the members had their choice of the volumes in rotation. He whose name stood, for that night, first on the list, had his choice of what volume he pleased in the whole collection; the second had his choice after the first; the third after the second, and so on to the last. At next meeting, he who had been first on the list at the preceding meeting, was last at this; he who had been second was first; and so on, through the whole three years. At the expiration of the engagement the books were sold by auction, but only among the members themselves; each man had his share of the common stock, in money or in books, as he chose to be a purchaser or not.

At the breaking up of this little society, which was formed under Mr. Riddell's patronage, what with benefactions of books from him, and what with their own purchase, they had collected together upwards of one hundred and fifty volumes. It will easily be guessed, that a good deal of trash would be bought. Among the books, however, of this little library were Blair's Sermons, Robertson's History of Scotland, Hume's History of the Stewarts, "The Spectator," "Idler," "Adventurer," "Mirror," "Lounger," "Observer," "Man of Feeling," "Man of the World," "Chrysal," "Don Quixote," "Joseph Andrews," &c. A peasant who can read and enjoy such books is certainly a much superior being to his neighbour who, perhaps, stalks beside his team very little removed, except in shape, from the brutes he drives.

Wishing your patriotic excertions their so much merited success,

    I am, Sir,
        Your humble Servant.
            A PEASANT

Letter from Burns to Sir John Sinclair, 1791

```
              THEATRE, DUMFRIES.
                  For the BENEFIT of
               Miſs FONTENELLE.
        On Wedneſday Dec. 4, 1793, will be preſented,
            A Comic Opera (never acted here) called
               THE HAUNTED TOWER.
             Written by Mr Cobb; Muſic by Storace.
               Baron of Oakland,     Mr Scriven,
               Lord William,         Mr Clarke,
               And Lord Edward,      Mr Williamſon.
                  Lady Elenor,      Miſs Harley,
                  And Adela,        Miſs Fontenelle.
               End of act 2d, a new Scots Air called
                      THE BANKS OF NITH.
          The words by Mr Burns; the muſic by Robert
            Riddell of Glenriddell, Eſq.—To be ſung by
          Miſs Fontenelle.
                        End of the Play,
               A NEW OCCASIONAL ADDRESS.
          Written by Mr Burns, to be ſpoken by Miſs
                           Fonteuelle.
          To which will be added (by particular deſire)
                    A Muſical Farce, called
                THE VIRGIN UNMASK'D.
                  Lucy,           Miſs Fontenelle.
                After which will be performed,
                    A Grand Spectacle, called
                  The Siege of Valenciennes.
          Founded on a ſeries of intereſting events, in the
          late operations of the combined armies on the
          Continent. Accompanied by Machinery and
          Action.
```

(71) Dumfries Weekly Journal, 1793

TO MISS FONTENELLE, Dumfries

Madam,
    In such a bad world as ours, those who add to the scanty sum of our pleasures are positively our benefactors. To you, Madam, on our humble Dumfries boards, I have been more indebted for entertainment than ever I was in prouder theatres. Your charms as a woman would ensure applause to the most indifferent actress, and your theatrical talents would ensure admiration to the plainest figure. This, Madam, is not the unmeaning or insidious compliment of the frivolous or the interested: I pay it from the same honest impulse that the sublime in nature excites my admiration, or her beauties give me delight.
    I have the honour to be, &c.- R.B.

Letter from Burns to Miss Fontenelle, 1792

I inclose you some copies of a couple of political ballads; one of which, I believe, you have never seen. Would to heaven I could make you master of as many votes in the Stewartry... In order to bring my humble efforts to bear with more effect on the foe, I have privately printed a good many copies of both ballads, and have sent them among friends all about the country.

Letter from Burns to Patrick Heron, 1795

Wham will we send to London town,
  To Parliament, and a' that,
Wha maist in a' the country round,
  For worth and sense may fa' that.-
    For a' that, and a' that,
      Thro' Galloway and a' that,
    Whilk is the Laird, or belted Knight,
      That best deserves to fa' that?

Wha sees Kirouchtree's open yett,
  And wha' is 't never saw that,
Or wha e'er wi' Kirouchtree met,
  That has a doubt of a' that?
    For a' that and a' that,
      Here's Heron yet for a' that;
    The independant Patriot,
      The Honest Man, an a' that.

from 'The Heron Ballads'

DUMFRIES, MARCH 24.
Yesterday came on at Kirkcudbright the election of a Member of Parliament for the stewartry of Kirkcudbright, when Patrick Heron of Heron, Esq. was elected by a majority of 21.

(72) Dumfries Weekly Journal, 1795

Robert Burns: Reflections of an Age

Dear Brother

It will be no very pleasing news to you to be told that I am dangerously ill, & not likely to get better. — An inveterate rheumatism has reduced me to such a state of debility, & my appetite is totally gone, so that I can scarce stand on my legs. — I have been a week at sea-bathing, & I will continue there or in a friend's house in the country all the summer. — God help my wife & children, if I am taken from their head! — They will be poor indeed. — I have contracted one or two serious debts, partly from my illness these many months & partly from too much thoughtlessness as to expense when I came to town that will cut in too much on the little I leave them in your hands. — Remember me to my Mother. — Yours

July 10th 1796.
R Burns

(73) Letter from Burns to his brother Gilbert, 1796

"Monday, 25th July.—This day at 12 o'clock went to the burial of Robert Burns, who died on the 21st, aged 38 years. In respect to the memory of such a genius as Mr Burns, his funeral was uncommonly splendid. The military here consisted of the Cinque Ports Cavelry and Angus-shire Fencibles, who, having handsomely tendered their services, lined the streets on both sides from the Court-house to the burial ground. (The corpse was carried from the place where Mr Burns died to the Court-house last night.) Order of procession : The firing party, which consisted of twenty of the Royal Dumfries Volunteers (of which Mr Burns was a member), in full uniform with crapes on the left arm, marched in front with their arms reversed, moving in a slow and solemn time to the 'Dead March' in Saul, which was played by the military band belonging to the Cinque Ports Cavalry. Next to the firing party was the band, then the bier or corpse supported by six of the Volunteers, who changed at intervals. The relations of the deceased and a number of the respectable inhabitants of both town and country followed next. Then the remainder of the Volunteers followed in rank, and the procession closed with a guard of Angus-shire Fencibles. The great bells of the churches tolled at intervals during the time of the procession. When arrived at the churchyard gate, the funeral party formed two lines, and leaned their heads on their firelocks pointed to the ground. Through this space the corpse was carried and borne to the grave. The party then drew up alongside of it, and fired three volleys over the coffin when deposited in the earth. Thus closed a ceremony which on the whole presented a solemn, grand, and affecting spectacle, and accorded with the general sorrow and regret for the loss of a man whose like we can scarce see again. As for his private character and behaviour, it might not have been so fair as could have been wished, but whatever faults he had I believe he was always worst for himself, and it becomes us to pass over his failings in silence, and with veneration and esteem look to his immortal works, which will live for ever. I believe his extraordinary genius may be said to have been the cause of bringing him so soon to his end, his company being courted by all ranks of people, and being of too easy and accommodating a temper, which often involved him in scenes of dissipation and intoxication, which by slow degrees impaired his health, and at last totally ruined his constitution. For originality of wit, rapidity of conception, and fluency of nervous phraseology he was unrivalled. He has left a wife and five children in very indigent circumstances, but I understand very liberal and extensive subscriptions are to be made for them. His wife was delivered of a child about an hour after he was removed from the house."

(74) Funeral of Robert Burns, 25th July 1796

Sources

1. Tytler's History of Scotland (Mackenzie, c 1850)
2. Tytler's History of Scotland (Mackenzie, c 1850)
3. Glasgow Weekly Herald, 26.1.1935
4. Statistical Account of Scotland (Creech, 1790s)
5. Glasgow Weekly Herald, 26.1.1935
6. Statistical Account of Scotland (Creech, 1790s)
7. The Land of Burns (Blackie & Son, 1840)
8. Statistical Account of Scotland (Creech, 1790s)
9. The Land of Burns (Blackie & Son, 1840)
10. Statistical Account of Scotland (Creech, 1790s)
11. Social Life in Scotland in the Eighteenth Century - H G Graham (A & C Black, 1909)
12. New Abbey Kirk Session Records, 17.5.1790
13. Social Life in Scotland in the Eighteenth Century - H G Graham (A & C Black, 1909)
14. Robert Burns: Rare Prints Collection (R G Kennedy & Co, 1900)
15. The Complete Works of Robert Burns (Thomas C Jack, c1835)
16. Robert Burns: Rare Prints Collection (R G Kennedy & Co, 1900)
17. Poetry of Robert Burns (Caxton Publishing, c1897)
18. The National Burns (William Mackenzie, 1879)
19. Encyclopædia Britannica (A& C Black,1875)
20. Robert Burns as a Freemason - W Harvey, 1921
21. Complete Works and Letters Masonic Edition, [1928]
22. Complete Works and Letters Masonic Edition, [1928]
23. War and Peace - L Tolstoy (Heinemann, 1911)
24. The Land of Burns (Blackie & Son, 1840)
25. The Land of Burns (Blackie & Son, 1840)
26. Old and New Edinburgh (Cassell, c1882)
27. The Land of Burns (Blackie & Son, 1840)
28. The Land of Burns (Blackie & Son, 1840)
29. Social Life in Scotland in the Eighteenth Century - H G Graham (A & C Black, 1909)
30. Tytler's History of Scotland (Mackenzie, c 1850)
31. Complete Works and Letters Masonic Edition, [1928]
32. The Land of Burns (Blackie & Son, 1840)
33. The Land of Burns (Blackie & Son, 1840)
34. The National Burns (William Mackenzie, 1879)
35. Old and New Edinburgh (Cassell, c1882)
36. The Land of Burns (Blackie & Son, 1840)
37. The Land of Burns (Blackie & Son, 1840)
38. The Land of Burns (Blackie & Son, 1840)
39. Tytler's History of Scotland (Mackenzie, c1850)
40. Old and New Edinburgh (Cassell, c1882)
41. Biographical Dictionary of Eminent Scotsmen (Blackie and Son, 1870)
42. Biographical Dictionary of Eminent Scotsmen (Blackie and Son, 1870)
43. SMT Magazine incorporating Scottish Country Life (SMT Magazines, 1936)
44. Letter from Robert Anderson to James Currie, 1799
45. Social Life in Scotland in the Eighteenth Century - H G Graham (A & C Black, 1909)
46. Old and New Edinburgh (Cassell, c1882)
47. Old and New Edinburgh (Cassell, c1882)
48. The Complete Works of Robert Burns (Thomas C Jack, c1835)
49. Old and New Edinburgh (Cassell, c1882)
50. Smuggling in the Solway - J Maxwell Wood (Maxwell & Son, 1908)
51. Johnson's Dictionary (1755)
52. Burns:Excise Officer and Poet - J Sinton (Menzies, 1898)
53. Annals of the Parish - J Galt (Macmillan, 1903)
54. "Character Book" of the Scottish Excise Board
55. Robert Burns: Rare Prints Collection (R G Kennedy & Co, 1900)
56. Amendment Act 1787
57. Burns:Excise Officer and Poet - J Sinton (Menzies, 1898)
58. A Treatise of Human Nature - D Hume, 1739
59. The Social Contract and Discourses - J J Rousseau, 1762
60. Social Life in Scotland in the Eighteenth Century - H G Graham (A & C Black, 1909)
61. Dumfries Weekly Journal 28.7.1789
62. Dumfries Weekly Journal 17.2.1795
63. The Rights of Man - T Paine, 1791
64. The Complete Works of Robert Burns (Thomas C Jack, c1835)
65. Statistical Account of Scotland (Creech, 1790s)
66. The Land of Burns (Blackie & Son, 1840)
67. The Land of Burns (Blackie & Son, 1840)
68. History of the Burgh of Dumfries - W McDowall (A & C Black, 1867)
69. The Land of Burns (Blackie & Son, 1840)
70. Robert Burns: Rare Prints Collection (R G Kennedy & Co, 1900)
71. Dumfries Weekly Journal 30.11.1793
72. Dumfries Weekly Journal 24.3.1795
73. Robert Burns: Rare Prints Collection (R G Kennedy & Co, 1900)
74. Dumfries and Galloway Standard 13.5.1896